This Notebook Belongs To

----

www.ingramcontent.com/pod-product-compliance
Lightning Source LLC
Chambersburg PA
CBHW052036280526
45791CB00010B/2983
9781073187416